INTRO

A recent Facebook post reminded us: "It takes six to eight pallbearers to lift you up when you're deceased. Imagine what you could accomplish if you had six to eight people lifting you up while you are living."

We do! Whether it is our parents and family, our past teachers and catechists, various mentors, supportive friends or colleagues, faith-filled parishioners, or caring neighbors, people have lifted us up throughout our lives—and they continue to do so.

As Catholics, rooted in the awe-inspiring reality of the communion of saints, we know we are "surrounded by so great a cloud of witnesses" (Hebrews 12:1). As catechists in today's church, we have the assurance that we are surrounded by those who have lived, experienced, and shared the word of God throughout the centuries by their words and their lives.

What support, empowerment, and challenge that gives us! We stand on the shoulders of those who came before us, sharing the Good News. We are standing on a firm and fervent foundation. The awareness and experience of that gives us incredible support. Our task is to build on what we've been given, for even our gifts can often be traced back to the creativity, generosity, and foresight of others.

Thank God that we are a community, a communion of saints! In the words of African American mystical scholar Barbara Holmes, "I am connected to the past and the future by the ligatures of well-lived lives, the mysteries of 'beyondness,' and the memories and narratives that lovingly bind and support me."

In the following pages, you will meet canonized saints of the church from throughout the centuries; those who, in more recent times, are on the path to canonization within the church; and a litany of many who have recently gone ahead of us who may not be in the official canonization process but through their holy, selfless, committed lives have prepared the way for our journey in catechetical ministry today.

You are probably familiar with some of them; others, perhaps, you've never heard of.

Isn't that exciting! We are surrounded by so many on whose shoulders we stand.

We enter this journey of reflection in gratitude, in awe, and with deep commitment, echoing the words of Joan Puls in *Seek Treasures in Small Fields: Everyday Holiness*: "When you walk, be aware of those who walk alongside you, behind you, before you, of those on whose efforts you now stand. We are surrounded, says the writer of Hebrews, by a cloud of witnesses."

Wonderings to Ponder and Live Today

- As you read a few words about each person, how do they inspire you? What do they teach you?
- Which one(s) are your favorites? Why? Who else would you add?
- How will you use their lives of inspiration and dedication to do something today: to go deeper, to try new things, to imitate something they did?

Pray a prayer of appreciation (especially before and after each of your catechetical sessions) to these saints and mentors, invisible but real presences who accompany you on your spiritual journey.

St. Angela Merici

FEAST DAY: JANUARY 27

Angela Merici, an Italian religious educator and founder of the Ursuline Sisters, was bold in responding to people's needs.

At 20 years of age, Angela became concerned that many young girls had no education. Wanting to respond to the needs of families by providing solid Christian education for future wives and mothers, she opened her home and began to teach. She felt called by God to invite other women to devote their lives to the religious formation of young girls.

In 1524, during a journey to the Holy Land, Angela became blind. She enthusiastically continued her trip as if she could see. Traveling home, her sight was restored while she was praying in the same place where she had become blind. Angela believed that the message was to never shut her eyes to the needs she saw—to never shut her heart to God's call.

Deciding to make her little group more formal, in 1535 Angela organized twelve women dedicated to catechetical work. Four years later, the group had increased to twenty-eight. She formed them into the Company of St. Ursula (patroness of medieval universities and venerated as a leader of women).

This was different from other women's religious orders that existed then: single women consecrated to Christ, living in the world rather than in a monastery, believing it was important to teach girls in their own homes with their families.

This first teaching order of women in the church was recognized only after Angela's death, when her Rule was approved by Pope Paul III in 1544, making the Ursulines an official religious community of women with a teaching ministry.

An Inspiring Mentor for Us Today

St. Angela's life calls us to be bold, never blind to people's needs. What are the needs of today? As catechists, we have the unique opportunity to touch lives: the lives of our learners and their families. All we do influences not just today but their lives in the years to come.

In her brief Rule, Angela nudged her companions to obey "divine inspirations that you may recognize them as coming from the Holy Spirit." When you see the needs of our learners and are prompted to respond (even with what may seem to be insignificant words and actions), recognize them as nudgings from the Spirit.

Wonderings to Ponder and Live Today

- Our ministry is not just to our learners but also to their families. How do you let parents/families know that you care about them?
- What bold steps do you take to nurture the faith of every family member?
- How do you get to know the life circumstances and needs of your learners and their families? How often do you call them (just to tell them you're thinking of them) or invite them to your sessions (and talk with them afterward)?
- What are the many ways that you connect God's story to your learners' life stories?
- What gift of the Holy Spirit would strengthen you to be a little bit bolder?

Black Elk

In November 2020, the U.S. bishops gave their support to the sainthood cause of Nicholas W. Black Elk, a 19th-century Lakota catechist who introduced hundreds of Lakota people to the Catholic faith.

During the 1860s, Black Elk was born into a lineage of medicine men, growing up participating in indigenous religion. A healer and visionary at a young age, he became curious about Christianity. His curiosity led him to watch and study.

During a Lakota healing ceremony for a boy's healing in 1904, Black Elk met a Jesuit who invited him to study Christianity. Black Elk was baptized Nicholas William on December 6, the Feast of St. Nicholas.

In 1907, the Jesuits appointed him a catechist because of his enthusiastic curiosity and excellent memory for learning Scripture and church teachings. He traveled widely, preaching and telling stories, writing pastoral letters in Lakota with Bible verses on good Christian living that newspapers published for people to read.

His life was integrated, intertwining his heritage as a Lakota medicine man and his call as a Catholic catechist. He used both his pipe and his rosary on a regular basis while praying, and he participated in eucharistic liturgies and Lakota ceremonies.

An Inspiring Mentor for Us Today

Black Elk could be named many things: a modern mystic, a catechist, a bridge builder. For us today, we are reminded that he did all these things—faithfully and passionately—because of his inquiring curiosity. Curious people ask questions, read, and explore. They actively seek information and life's varied experiences and are willing to meet challenges and broaden their horizons. They are not shy about asking questions and delving deeply into the mysteries and truths of life.

The very vocation of catechist calls each of us to a life of faith-filled, wonder-filled curiosity. A limitless inquisitiveness about people (especially our learners and their families), all of God's world, and the Holy Mystery of our God leads us to discover, celebrate, and share the faith, hope, and love that God showers on us, our learners, and the world.

As we live out our call to echo the Good News and challenge of Jesus' life, new questions and wonderments will always emerge, filling us with the peace, strength, and eagerness to grow in our faithful relationship with God and share our God-experiences by the way we live and catechize.

Wonderings to Ponder and Live Today

- What are you curious about when it comes to life and faith? How might you find new answers and experiences?
- If you committed to learn something new every day about our faith, about God's created world, what might you watch for or search out?
- Use "I wonder..." questions with your learners (rather than just what, when, and where questions).
- When your learners raise a question, try asking for their thoughts before answering.
- Use open-ended stories. Ask your learners for their opinion on how stories might end, encouraging them to think of many possibilities.

Blesseds Daudi Okelo and Jildo Irwa

FEAST DAY: OCTOBER 20

In 2002, St. John Paul II celebrated the beatification of 16-year-old Daudi Okelo and 12-year-old Jildo Irwa, catechists who, in 1916, traveled into a region of Uganda to teach the faith to the local people.

Daudi and Jildo, members of the Acholi people of northern Uganda, were born into pagan families. Educated by the Comboni Missionaries, they were baptized in 1916. Daudi became a catechist the next year, with Jildo as his assistant, as they strove to serve especially the poor.

Each day at dawn, they beat the drum to call the catechumens to morning prayer. They taught the prayers and the catechism's answers. At sunset, they gathered the villagers for common prayer and the rosary, closing with a Marian song. They also visited the nearby small villages to meet with the children who were busy during the day helping their parents look after the cattle or work in the fields.

Daudi was described as a young man of peaceful and shy character, diligent in his duties as a catechist and loved by all. He never got involved in tribal or political disputes, which were fairly frequent at that time. Jildo, with a lively and gentle nature, was quite intelligent. He knew how to entertain the children with village games and joyful gatherings. Always available, he was loved by everyone and admired for his duties as assistant catechist.

People who opposed the new religion took advantage of the socio-political unrest in the area to stop the preaching of the gospel. Daudi and Jildo were hounded, threatened, ordered to give up their activities, and finally speared to death.

Inspiring Mentors for Us Today

These two young catechists inspire us in our ministry today in many ways. Certainly, they are courageous models of a challenge we don't face: giving their lives rather than abandoning their ministry of catechesis. By fearlessly moving to a place outside their own ethnic clan, they are a sign of the catholicity and unity of the church. Having just celebrated baptism and confirmation, they realized that to be a Christian means to share one's faith; they started their work as catechists at once.

They remind us, too, that people are never too young to begin sharing and echoing the Good News. They also model for us the power and strength of ministering together.

Wonderings to Ponder and Live Today

- Is there a young person in your parish whom you could invite to be a catechist helper with you—or to do one-time things, such as music or service leader?
- What are some ways you can collaborate with other catechists in your parish: planning together, sharing resources, team teaching, inviting older learners to adopt a younger learner, and so on?
- Just as Daudi and Jildo moved outside of their clan, how might you and your learners connect with learners in other parishes in your diocese or in other places around the world?
- How might you help your learners learn about Catholics throughout the world?

St. Catherine of Siena

FEAST DAY: APRIL 29

Catherine was born in Siena, Italy, in 1347 as the Black Death was ravaging Afro-Eurasia. She was the twenty-fifth child in her family (although half of her brothers and sisters did not survive childhood).

From an early age, Catherine wanted no part of marriage but planned to devote herself to God. She became a Third Order Dominican when she was 18 and spent the next three years in seclusion and prayer. When she felt called by God to help others, she combined her contemplation with action. She visited the poor and sick in their homes and in the hospital. Her activities quickly attracted followers who helped in her mission to serve others.

Catherine was soon drawn into more active involvement in the religious struggles of the time. The Great Schism split Christendom between two, then three, popes. Catherine traveled, calling for reform of the church and for people to love God totally. Her influence with Pope Gregory XI played a role in his decision to leave Avignon and return to Rome. He then entrusted her with many missions of brokering peace deals during a time of conflict between the Italian city-states, which was rare for a woman at this time.

Physical travel was not the only way in which Catherine influenced people. She composed over four hundred letters, her Dialogue (conversations she had with God), and prayers. These works were so influential that she was declared a Doctor of the Church.

Catherine's letters are considered one of the great works of early Italian literature. In addition to writing to her friends, she wrote to popes, Blessed Raymond of Capua (her confessor), the kings of France and Hungary, the queen of Naples, and numerous religious figures. Her beginning letters were mostly encouragement and teaching for her followers but then began to address the day's challenges, begging for peace and reform of the church.

Twenty-six of her prayers also survive, mostly composed in the last eighteen months of her life.

An Inspiring Mentor for Us Today

There are many ways that Catherine is a model for us today: her intimate relationship with Christ; her belief that holiness is the journey of life; her work for church unity; her courage to speak truth.

Perhaps, though, as catechists today, we might imitate Catherine in a very practical way: by writing—letters, composing prayers, keeping a journal of our faith life.

Wonderings to Ponder and Live Today

- Do you keep a journal of your faith/life experiences—your conversations with God? Might you begin to keep a journal of the God-moments in your catechetical ministry?
- Have you ever written down your prayers, especially your prayers for your learners and their families? Have you shared these prayers with them? Give it a try.
- Take time throughout the year to snail-mail a letter to each of your learners, affirming them and reminding them of God's unique care for them in their interests and needs.
- Do you stay in touch with your past learners through periodic letters of support, inspiration, and prayer? If not, is this something you could do?

St. Charles Borromeo

FEAST DAY: NOVEMBER 4

Charles Borromeo (1538–1584), a lawyer, teacher, pastor, cardinal, holy man, and reformer, influenced the renewal of the church in the final years of the Council of Trent.

In 1559, when his uncle, Cardinal de Medici, was elected Pope Pius IV, he made Charles (a layman) cardinal-deacon and administrator of the Archdiocese of Milan. Charles was later ordained at the age of 25 and consecrated bishop of Milan.

The pope, though, kept him in Rome performing various functions. The Council of Trent had been suspended for ten years; Borromeo encouraged the pope to reopen the council in 1562. With direction from that council, Borromeo supervised the writing of an accurate catechism, rewrote liturgical texts and music, and began enforcing clerical reform in Rome.

Finally able to move to his diocese of Milan, he began preaching, wandered the city praying with the people, and changed the way that the church listened to the people. He established hospitals, colleges, orphanages, and other charitable institutions. To teach religion to children, Borromeo established a confraternity of Christian doctrine in every parish in his diocese; this organization grew to include 740 schools, 3,000 catechists, and 40,000 students in Sunday schools.

Unlike the civil authorities, who fled during the plague and famine of 1576, Borromeo stayed in the city, ministering to the sick and dying and helping those in want. He borrowed large sums of money that required years to repay so he could feed 60,000 to 70,000 people daily.

An Inspiring Mentor for Us Today

Along with St. Robert Bellarmine, Borromeo has been named patron of catechists. Some of his biographers have said that Borromeo's work "gave new confidence to a shaken church." Here is a job description for each of us as catechists: to bring resilience and hope to a shaken church and a suffering world.

In the homily during his installation Mass, Pope Francis prompted us: "Today amid so much darkness we need to see the light of hope and to be men and women who bring hope to others." Theologian and philosopher Pierre Teilhard de Chardin said, "The future belongs to those who give the next generation reason for hope."

In our hurting, searching world, what greater gift to share with our learners than a genuine spirit of hope, commitment, and enthusiasm because we know—no, more than that, we have experienced—God's love in us, with us, around us, through us.

Wonderings to Ponder and Live Today

- Who is a person of hope for you? Who touches your life with hope? To whom do you go to find hope?
- What brings you the most hope these days?
- When and how does your enthusiasm show through: in how you pray with your learners? in how you talk about God with them? in the way you respond to and care for your learners? in the activities and experiences during your learning sessions?
- How are you a person of hope for others? What might you do to cultivate a spirit of hope? How do you encourage your learners to bring resilience and hope to our hurting world?

St. Dominic

FEAST DAY: AUGUST 8

Born in Spain in 1170, Dominic studied the arts and theology, was ordained, and became a canon of the cathedral at Osma. On a journey through France with his bishop, Dominic encountered the Albigensians, heretics who denied the Incarnation and the validity of the sacraments.

Dominic was commissioned to be part of the preaching crusade against the heresy. He and his followers—in their simplicity, poverty, and contemplative prayer—were in contrast to other preachers of the time who stayed at the best inns and employed servants.

Because the nobility needed a place to educate their children and Catholic women needed a safe place away from hostile heretics, Dominic established a convent at Prouille in 1206, which would become the first Dominican house.

In July 1215, Dominic was granted permission to form a religious order. These men traveled the countryside to preach and set up a system of education. The order was confirmed in 1216; in 1217, Pope Honorius III dubbed Dominic and his followers "The Order of Preachers." Shortly after, the pope elevated Dominic to Master of the Sacred Palace. The position has been occupied by Dominican preachers ever since.

An Inspiring Mentor for Us Today

Flowing from Dominic's life, the Dominican motto is *contemplata aliis tradere*, the passing on to others what one has encountered in contemplation. As a preacher, Dominic was a catechist. His preaching was rooted in his contemplative life: study, prayer, and quiet with God. An active contemplative life isn't just for those in convents and monasteries. We, as catechists, are called to be contemplative activists. How would we have anything to give to others if we first had not lived in God's presence through prayer and quiet?

We do much today (and rightly so!) to motivate young people toward Christian service. That is easier when we lead our learners to do it the way Jesus and Dominic did: rooted in prayer and silence, which allows God to deepen our sense of gratitude and openness to the gift of each moment of life.

Wonderings to Ponder and Live Today

- Reflect upon the place of silence and quiet in your life:
    - » How much time do you allow each day for prayer? Do you do all the talking?
    - » When you have some free time, do you find yourself at your computer, on your phone, or in front of the TV, or do you sometimes read, pray, rest in God's presence?
- Do you begin your sessions with centering or quieting exercises which help your learners bridge the gap between their noisy world and this graced time?
- How do you develop prayer services (and moments in the catechetical session) where there is time for quiet spaces?
- Contemplation connects us with others and inspires us to action. Often, we have interpreted contemplation to mean a withdrawal from people and activity. Nothing is further from the truth. There is nothing passive about the contemplative way of life. Rather, it is the still point that grounds meaning in authentic action. How do you connect contemplation and action/service for your learners?

Dorothy Day

In 2000, after New York City's Cardinal John O'Connor formally requested that the Congregation for the Causes of Saints in Rome consider Dorothy Day's canonization, she was officially named a "Servant of God."

Dorothy's cause for sainthood was officially endorsed, with overwhelming support, by the U.S. Conference of Catholic Bishops in 2012. In 2021, the diocesan phase (a biographical presentation) was completed and sent to the Vatican, which began the Roman phase (toward naming Dorothy venerable).

Peter Maurin, a French peasant-philosopher, convinced Dorothy in 1933 to publish a newspaper, *The Catholic Worker*, to disseminate the far-reaching implications and challenges of the gospel. Rather than just theoretically advocating for social justice, the articles focused on the possibilities, they described what society would look like if it were organized around values of solidarity, community, and human dignity instead of selfishness and greed.

Believing it was not enough to just write about these ideas, Day and Maurin desired to live them. This led to the opening of houses of hospitality to live the works of mercy: feeding the hungry, sheltering the homeless. Even that wasn't enough for Dorothy. Beyond caring for the poor, she knew it was essential to challenge the social structures that cause poverty. The standard that guided her was the Sermon on the Mount and the conviction that what we do for the poor we do directly for Christ.

In 2015, when Pope Francis visited the United States, he included Dorothy as one of the "four great Americans" he named in his speech to Congress. Today, 187 Catholic Worker communities remain committed to nonviolence, voluntary poverty, prayer, and hospitality for the homeless, exiled, hungry, and forsaken.

Catholic Workers continue to protest injustice, war, racism, and violence in all forms.

An Inspiring Mentor for Us Today

Dorothy Day is not usually thought of as a patron saint of catechists, and yet, her life is the epitome of one who echoes the Good News as well as one who lives what she believes. Dorothy taught the social teachings of the church by her words; she personified the challenge of the gospel by her life.

Dorothy's words catechized many through her 721 articles in *The Catholic Worker* from 1933 until her death in 1980, as well as many articles in other publications. Dorothy was a model of discipleship, through her passion teaching others actions for justice, especially for the oppressed.

Wonderings to Ponder and Live Today

- Is there one social justice teaching of the church which is especially important to you?
- How do you help learners discern their gifts and talents and how they may be used to serve others?
- Have you ever used the life of a saint or a modern-day person to illustrate the benefits of leading a simpler lifestyle?
- How might we catechize our learners about our call to respond with the two feet of service: charity and social justice/advocacy?
- How can you involve the families of your learners in a social justice-themed project?

St. Elizabeth Ann Seton

FEAST DAY: JANUARY 4

A wife, mother, widow, and friend, Elizabeth Ann Seton was the first American to be canonized as a saint.

In 1774, Elizabeth Ann Bayley was born into a prominent New York Episcopalian family; at the age of three, she lost her mother. When she was 19, Elizabeth married William Seton, a wealthy businessman, with whom she had five children. The couple traveled to Italy in 1803 to get help for William's tuberculosis, where Elizabeth discovered and was intrigued by Catholicism. After William's death, Elizabeth returned to the United States and entered the Catholic Church in 1805.

After several difficult years, widowed and penniless, Elizabeth moved in 1809 to Emmitsburg, Maryland, where she opened a school for girls. Women from throughout the country came to join her and, over time, they formally began their religious life as Sisters of Charity.

Although Elizabeth died at the young age of 46, she left a legacy for the church and catechetical ministry (while also raising her five children). The Sisters of Charity was the first American religious community for women. Her school for girls was the first American parish school, planting the seeds of Catholic education in the United States. She also established the first American Catholic orphanage. Her Sisters of Charity now minister throughout North America, responding to the unmet needs of people in poverty.

An Inspiring Mentor for Us Today

One of the realities that led Elizabeth to Catholicism and guided her life was the mystery and gift of Jesus' presence with us in the Eucharist.

Our spirituality as catechists is centered in the Eucharist because of the challenge of what Eucharist is: in receiving the Body of Christ, we become the body of Christ. There is an implication, a challenge, for us in that.

Our Eucharist-centered spirituality impels us to do, in memory of Jesus, exactly what he did: to be broken and poured out in nourishment, to be a servant to others, to wash the feet of others. Especially for us as catechists, because we have celebrated Eucharist, we are the presence of Jesus in our world. We wash feet; we nourish others in the beliefs we share, in the gospel values we live.

Wonderings to Ponder and Live Today

- When are some times (during liturgy as well as during your 24/7 life) that you are most aware of being the Body of Christ?
- When you say "Amen" as you receive the Eucharist, what are you saying "Amen" to?
- The author Annie Dillard wrote that we don't have the foggiest idea of the power of the Eucharist. She advises in her book *Teaching a Stone to Talk* that we wear crash helmets and seat belts in the pews because what we celebrate is life-changing and life-shaking. What is the power of the Eucharist for you?
- As a catechist, when do you give your life as nourishment for others?
- Catechesis for Eucharist doesn't occur only before First Communion. How do you help your learners deepen their understanding of the Eucharist?

St. Hildegard of Bingen

FEAST DAY: SEPTEMBER 17

Hildegard, a medieval (1098–1179) mystic, composer, author, preacher, poet, playwright, and Benedictine nun, was canonized in 2012 and named a Doctor of the Church (the fourth woman of thirty-five saints to be given that title by the Catholic Church). Pope Benedict XVI described Hildegard as "perennially relevant" and "an authentic teacher of theology and a profound scholar of natural science and music" (St. Peter's Square, May 27, 2012).

Having had visions since she was three years old, Hildegard was ordered by her confessor to write them down. When Pope Eugene III read them, he encouraged her to continue. In addition to these, she wrote commentaries on the gospels, the Athanasian Creed, and the Rule of St. Benedict, as well as lives of the saints and a medical work on the well-being of the body. She wrote over three hundred letters to people who sought her advice.

Hildegard carried out four preaching missions in northern Europe (an unprecedented activity for a woman in that time). She did not hesitate to call out religious leaders who were corrupt, authorities who abused their power, and people in religious life who created an easy way of life rather than going into their communities and working with the people they were called to serve.

Pope Benedict XVI said, "Let us always invoke the Holy Spirit, so that he may inspire in the Church holy and courageous women like Saint Hildegard of Bingen who, developing the gifts they have received from God, make their own special and valuable contribution to the spiritual development of our communities and of the Church in our time" (General Audience, September 8, 2010).

An Inspiring Mentor for Us Today

Hildegard is a witness for us as catechists in her numerous roles: artist, author, composer, mystic, pharmacist, poet, preacher, theologian.

Perhaps one that is especially pertinent for us today is seen in one of the themes that occur constantly in her writings and prayer: the stewardship of creation and holistic living. Hildegard valued the earth as a place of wonder, of delight and glory to God.

She communicated creation spirituality through music, art, poetry, medicine, gardening, and reflections on nature. Hildegard coined the word *viriditas* or "greenness" to describe the reality of God's presence in all living things. She had visions of air pollution and deforestation centuries before either became an issue, and she held a strong conviction that the job of humans was to cherish and protect the world they live in.

Wonderings to Ponder and Live Today

- How do you help your learners understand science as a revelation of the mysteries and glories of God's creation?
- How might you incorporate care for creation into prayer time with your learners?
- Within your catechetical settings, how might you reject our throwaway culture?
- Is there a care for creation project in your local community that your learners might participate in as a group throughout your year together?

St. Jerome

FEAST DAY: SEPTEMBER 30

It has been said that there is no one who has had greater influence on the way Catholics read Scripture than St. Jerome.

Born into a rich family around 347 in what is now Yugoslavia, Jerome was educated in Rome, learning Latin and Greek and becoming a lawyer. Toward the end of his schooling, he converted and was baptized. His experiences were many: traveling to the east, studying Hebrew and spending four years as a hermit in Antioch; after ordination, going to Constantinople to study Scripture under St. Gregory Nazianzen; traveling extensively in Palestine, marking each spot of Christ's life; as a mystic, spending five years in the desert of Chalcis in prayer, penance, and study.

In 382, Jerome became secretary to Pope Damasus, who commissioned him to translate the Hebrew text of the Bible. He settled in Bethlehem, where he lived as a semi-recluse in the cave believed to have been the birthplace of Christ, translating and writing for his last 34 years. His translation of the Bible into the form of Latin most commonly read at the time (the Vulgate) was his greatest gift to the church. Jerome's desire was that the word of God would be readily available to everyone in a language they understood. The Vulgate brought the Scriptures out of the churches and into everyday life; the Latin Vulgate is still the official Latin Bible of the Catholic Church.

In addition to the translation, Jerome wrote on varied topics, including commentary on all the prophets and many books of the Bible, some history, and a few biographies. He also founded a school for boys and served as a spiritual guide for the monks and nuns who settled in Bethlehem to be near him. He gave shelter to refugees who came to the Holy Land following the sack of Rome by the Vandals in 410.

Saints and Mentors for Catechists

An Inspiring Mentor for Us Today

St. Jerome said (and lived), "Ignorance of the Scriptures is ignorance of Christ." As catechists, we have received and we pass on not just a message, but a person: Jesus who lived among us and remains with us. In Scripture, we hear the constant invitation to be united with God, to live as Jesus did.

Our sessions with our learners are vibrant and engaging when they flow from the word of God, from the word of Life, which call us to live a life of wisdom and hope, compassion and forgiveness, reverence and awe, love and service.

Wonderings to Ponder and Live Today

- Do you have a favorite book or quote from Scripture? What makes this a favorite?
- How would you complete this sentence: "As a result of my time studying God's word, I will..."
- Have you prayed with *lectio divina* (sacred reading)? How might you invite your learners to this method of prayer?
- What methods do you use to help Scripture come alive for your learners (guided meditation, role playing, open-ended stories, rewriting passages, etc.)?

John Baptist de la Salle

FEAST DAY: APRIL 7

Born into a wealthy family in 1651, John Baptist de la Salle was named canon of Reims Cathedral in France when he was 16 and ordained to the priesthood at the age of 26.

In his day, only the rich could afford an education for their children. Moved by the needs of the poor, John determined to put his talents and advanced education at their service. Totally dedicated, he abandoned his family home, moved in with the teachers, renounced his position as canon and his wealth, and formed the community that became known as the Brothers of the Christian Schools (Christian Brothers).

John Baptist de la Salle was an educational innovator, often going against the norms of the day (which brought opposition and criticism from church and public authorities). He and his brothers created a network of quality free-of-charge schools throughout France devoted to teaching poor children that featured instruction in the local language (rather than Latin), students grouped according to ability and achievement, integration of religious instruction with secular subjects, and the involvement of parents.

They offered Sunday courses for working young men and founded technical schools; secondary schools for modern languages, arts, and sciences; and one of the first institutions in France for the care of delinquents. John was insistent on the preparation of lay teachers in a first-of-its-kind teacher training college, forming well-prepared teachers with a sense of vocation and mission.

John's vision was that, in the eyes of God, working-class children were just as important and had as much right to education as the children of the king.

For years, church authorities resisted his creation of a new form of religious life: a community of men dedicated exclusively to education, with no ordained members.

An Inspiring Mentor for Us Today

St. John Baptist de la Salle was an exemplary teacher who had innovative and effective ideas on how to educate youth, meeting the unique challenges of his day. As catechists, we are impelled by today's needs to dream, to innovate, and to implement creative and prophetic catechetical approaches.

How are we designing program structures that respond to the experiences of today's families? How do we implement faith formation as year-round, involving the whole community, and lifelong? Are we educating for the reign of God rather than just about the church? What would it look like if we shifted from an academic model to a relational model? How do we adopt new models that meet today's needs, answer today's questions, and respect all cultures?

Wonderings to Ponder and Live Today

- What are the ways you are empowering families to be the domestic church they already are?
- In addition to learning the beliefs of our faith, how are you providing opportunities for people to encounter God?
- What might be some ways that you can help your learners (and their families) learn by serving?
- How do you infuse Catholic Social Teaching in all you do, empowering people to work for a just world?
- How are you using the best methods possible, integrating in-person and virtual learning?

St. John Bosco

FEAST DAY: JANUARY 31

During his youth, John Bosco was encouraged to be ordained so he could work with young boys. His care for young people began when he met a poor orphan and instructed him in preparation for Holy Communion.

John's ministry was in Turin, Italy, a city in the throes of industrialization, including slums and widespread poverty. He met young men and boys where they worked and played. He used his talents as a performer, doing magic tricks to capture attention, then sharing with the children his message for the day.

At a time when harsh corporal punishment was the norm, John Bosco imitated the gentleness of Christ. His educational style was based on reason, religion, and loving kindness (the Preventive System). He led young people to the study of the faith and to apostolic, civil, and professional commitment.

With Pope Pius IX's encouragement, John founded the Society of St. Francis de Sales (Salesians) in 1859. Their activity concentrated on education, faith formation, and mission work. Later, he organized a group of Salesian Sisters to assist girls.

John Bosco's ministry responded to the needs of the whole person: he sought work for boys who needed it and searched for lodgings for others. By the 1860s, he and his mother were responsible for lodging eight hundred boys. He is one of the pioneers of Mutual Aid Societies, initiated as collaborative financial support to young migrant Catholic workers in Turin. He drew up regulations to assist apprentices when any of them was without work or fell ill.

He also used various methods to teach: for example, he purchased a printing press to publish catechetical pamphlets. In 1875, he launched the *Salesian Bulletin*, currently published in fifty editions and thirty languages.

An Inspiring Mentor for Us Today

In one of his letters (which appears in the Office of Readings for his January 31 feast day), John Bosco wrote: "Let us regard those boys over whom we have some authority as our own sons.... There must be no hostility in our minds, no contempt in our eyes, no insult on our lips. We must use mercy for the present and have hope for the future, as is fitting for true fathers who are eager for real correction and improvement."

An important reminder for us as catechists today! Do our learners and their families hear only affirmations from us and always see respect and compassion in our eyes?

Wonderings to Ponder and Live Today

- As you think about your learners as your daughters and sons, what is your hope and dream for them?
- Do you greet each learner as they enter your meeting space each week with a smile and welcome? Do you remember what is happening in their lives, their activities, their interests?
- How do you accept your learners as they are as well as nudging them to grow to be even more who God created them to be?
- How might you encourage and empower your learners to be people of care and encouragement for others?

St. John Leonardi

FEAST DAY: OCTOBER 9

Living at a time of great reformation in the church (after the Protestant Reformation and the Council of Trent), Leonardi was trained to be a pharmacist. He soon, however, turned to the study of theology and preparation for ordination.

Following ordination, Leonardi ministered often in hospitals and prisons. The example and dedication of his work attracted several young men who began to assist him. They organized a communal form of life and began the process that led to the formation of the Order of the Mother of God (also known as the Clerks Regular of the Mother of God).

Dedicated to the spirit of the Catholic Counter-Reformation launched by the Council of Trent, John Leonardi and his congregation of priests sought to deepen the knowledge and practice of the faith among clergy and laity. In a letter written to Pope Paul V, he stressed the universal call to holiness of life for all members of the church.

Preaching about this call to holiness, Leonardi believed passionately in the religious instruction of the young. He worked with young people through the Confraternity of Christian doctrine and published a compendium of Christian doctrine that remained in use until the 19th century. He also established a society of priests dedicated to working in foreign missions, which became the Society for the Propagation of the Faith.

John Leonardi died in Rome in 1609 after contracting a deadly illness while caring for victims of a plague outbreak. He was canonized in 1938.

An Inspiring Mentor for Us Today

In a letter to Pope Paul V, John Leonardi wrote: "Nothing should be left untried that can train children from early childhood in good morals and in the earnest practice of Christianity."

Pope Francis continually echoes those thoughts. In November 2019, during a visit to Thailand, he said, "We need to seek new ways of spreading the word, ways that are capable of mobilizing and awakening a desire to know the Lord." In his 2021 document *Instituting the Ministry of Catechist*, Pope Francis again calls catechists to be open to new ways of preaching and sharing the Good News of the gospel.

Wonderings to Ponder and Live Today

- In the last three years of your catechetical ministry, what new approaches/methods have you used?
- What would you like to do now? What might be stopping you?
- Instead of using the same type of activities in each session, do you invite the learners to respond through a new type of media, different materials, participative experiences?
- To invite learners to try new things (as well as respond with their interests and gifts), might you suggest options (rather than everyone doing the same thing)? For instance, while exploring prayer: using paint, show how you feel when praying alone, when praying with others; rewrite the Magnificat in your own words; design gestures to accompany your favorite psalm; select a popular song that can be used as prayer, creating a PowerPoint presentation to accompany it.

St. Katharine Drexel

FEAST DAY: MARCH 3

Katharine Drexel, who many believe started the Catholic Church in America on the road toward racial integration, was born into a wealthy Philadelphia banking family in 1858.

Her biographers relate that at her father's death, she became one of the richest people in America. Yet, despite her riches—using her riches—she focused her time, energy, and money on education and on racial justice.

Traveling the United States, she saw the difficult circumstances of Native Americans and African Americans. Following their father's death, Katharine and her sisters contributed money to the St. Francis Mission in South Dakota. Katharine became convinced that more people were needed to help the Native Americans. While touring Europe, she had a private audience with Pope Leo XIII, asking him to send missionaries to the Native American missions. "Why don't *you* become a missionary?" he asked.

After prayer, conversation with spiritual directors, and several years of training, she founded a missionary community, the Sisters of the Blessed Sacrament, whose special focus was the education of Native Americans and African Americans.

When she died at the age of 96 (in 1955), there were more than 500 members of her order, and they had opened 145 missions, 49 elementary schools, and 12 high schools as well as Xavier University in New Orleans, the first university in the country for African American students.

An Inspiring Mentor for Us Today

We might say that we can't identify with Katharine Drexel, thinking that she was able to accomplish all that she did because of her wealth. Yet, do we not have the riches of our talents, our generous love, our committed faith, and the blessings of the graces of our God?

Perhaps one of the greatest lessons we learn from Katharine is that the answer to challenges around us lies within ourselves. Pope Leo XIII, rather than sending more missionaries, called her to be that missionary. The next time we see one of our learners struggling, when our learners' families seem to need some nudging or comfort, when there seems to be something missing in our parish catechetical program or a problem in our neighborhood, community, or nation, rather than complaining, can we pray, asking for guidance on how we can be part of the solution?

Wonderings to Ponder and Live Today

- Being part of the solution means more than listening to the voices in our head. Whom do you listen to when you're trying to solve a challenge?
- We are part of the solution because we are a community. How do you help your learners understand the joys and the responsibilities of being community?
- Being part of God's family means there are many people who do not look like us. Is it possible to provide opportunities for your learners to learn more about others and to interact with them?
- Belonging to the community of God's family means that "we" is more important than "me." How do you help your learners live other-centered lives (in a me-first world)?

St. Mary Magdalene

FEAST DAY: JULY 22

Mentioned by name twelve times in the Gospels, Mary (from the town of Magdala on the Sea of Galilee) was one of a group of women who traveled with Jesus during his public ministry. (Mary Magdalene has often been regarded as sexually immoral, but this is not supported in Scripture.)

In all four gospels, Mary Magdalene was a witness to the crucifixion of Jesus and, in the synoptic gospels (Matthew, Mark, and Luke), she was also present at his burial. She was also the first one to see the empty tomb, having gone to care for the dead body of Jesus. Initially, she thought that his body had been stolen or was missing.

It was only when she personally encountered Jesus in the garden near the tomb and heard him call her by name that she understood that Jesus was alive. She was the first to touch Jesus after the resurrection, and the one chosen by Jesus to announce the good news to the apostles who were huddled in the upper room.

Mary Magdalene is recognized as a saint by the Catholic, Eastern Orthodox, Anglican, and Lutheran churches. In 2016, Pope Francis changed July 22 from a memorial to a feast, a day to be celebrated universally throughout the church on par with feasts of the apostles. He also called Mary the "Apostle to the Apostles," an ancient designation first used for her by St. Thomas Aquinas.

An Inspiring Mentor for Us Today

In Scripture, we never see Mary wavering in her support of Jesus. Perhaps her commitment is best seen in her actions in Jesus' final days. Through the agonizing hours of his crucifixion and the desolate Sabbath that followed, she holds her group of women together. On Sunday morning, she leads them once again: to the tomb for a reverential anointing.

In our daily lives, and perhaps at various times in our catechetical ministry, things just seem too difficult. We wonder: Am I making a difference? Does my time here really matter? I'm sure someone else could do this better. Is it time for me to just bow out of this ministry?

Mary Magdalene is a witness for us of steadfast dedication through the good times and the difficult times. Even though we might not—immediately or ever—see the fruit of our labors, we remain committed because of the person of Jesus.

Wonderings to Ponder and Live Today

- When things are difficult and you feel as though you'd like to walk away, what helps you to stay with them?
- Mary traveled with other women and the disciples. Who are companions for you on the journey?
- Mary was committed because of her relationship with Jesus. What helps you not just know *about* Jesus but deepen your relationship with Jesus?
- Mary did not waver because she remembered God's promises that Jesus taught. What promises in Scripture support and encourage you?
- How do you lead your learners to a relationship with Jesus in addition to knowing about him?

St. Robert Bellarmine

FEAST DAY: SEPTEMBER 17

When Pope Clement VIII named Robert Bellarmine a cardinal in 1599, he declared him to be the most educated man in the church. A brilliant scholar, professor of theology, homilist, writer, and papal theologian, Bellarmine taught about the Catholic faith during a time of many questions raised by the Protestant Reformation.

He helped implement the teachings of the Council of Trent and contributed many theological writings to the church. He wrote the three-volume *Disputations on the Controversies* (1581–1593), the earliest attempt to outline the religious controversies of the time and clearly explain the teachings of the Catholic Church. He also helped create the authoritative Latin text of the Bible asked for by the Council of Trent. In 1598, Bellarmine published a catechism that was still being used into the 20th century.

As a diocesan bishop, he was known for his dedication and skill in teaching the faith. One biographer shares that, during a time when sermons were common in Capua only during Advent and Lent, Bellarmine preached every Sunday and went to great trouble to travel to the remote areas of his diocese during the week to catechize his congregation.

Bellarmine lived a simple and humble life, having a compassionate love for the poor. Even when he was a cardinal, he ate only the food available to the poor. Once he used the hangings in his room to clothe poor people, saying, "The walls won't catch cold."

An Inspiring Mentor for Us Today

Certainly, St. Robert Bellarmine was named patron saint of catechists because he catechized many people (as we do) and because he wrote a catechism (which we don't do because we have Catholic publishers who provide us with exceptional materials). Perhaps most inspiring for us is Bellarmine's devotion to and love of learning, his thirst to know Scripture and the church's teachings. He looked upon learning as one of the ways of serving God and as an indispensable foundation for his teaching.

Countless opportunities surround us today to do what Bellarmine did to continue learning as we nurture our faith and our catechetical ministry: parish and (arch)diocesan catechist formation programs, online courses, frequent gatherings of the catechists in our parish (and/or region), retreats, faith-sharing and prayer groups, books and periodicals, days of reflection, workshops, seasonal parish and (arch)diocesan programs, Scripture study, service followed by reflection, and more.

Wonderings to Ponder and Live Today

- From whom have you learned about our faith? What did they do to enable you to learn, to grow, to be enthusiastic about the faith?
- Because of your experiences as a catechist—in your planning and teaching—what new insights have you learned about our faith, about deepening your relationship with Jesus?
- In which areas of your ministry do you feel best prepared? In which areas do you feel the need for more information and formation?
- As you continue on this journey, what are two or three things you would like to (or need to) continue to learn?

St. Rose Philippine Duchesne

FEAST DAY: NOVEMBER 18

Rose was born in Grenoble, France, in 1769, into a family that was among the new rich. At 19, she entered the Visitation of Mary convent; during the French Revolution, the convent was closed and the order expelled from France. She began caring for the poor and sick, opened a school for homeless children, and risked her life helping priests in the underground.

After the war, she entered the Religious of the Sacred Heart of Jesus, soon becoming superior and supervisor of the novitiate and a school. Having heard stories of missionary work in Louisiana when she was a little girl, her dream was to go to America and work among the Native Americans. When she was 49, Rose was sent to the United States, where she founded a boarding school for daughters of pioneers near St. Louis and opened the first free school for girls west of the Mississippi.

When she was 72, a school for the Potawatomi was opened in Kansas. Many thought Rose was too sick to go, but the Jesuit head of the mission insisted: "She must come; she may not be able to do much work, but she will assure success to the mission by praying for us."

Her health did prevent her from taking an active role, but her long hours of prayer impelled the Native Americans to name her *Quah-kah-ka-num-ad*, "Woman Who Prays Always."

An Inspiring Mentor for Us Today

We might look to St. Rose Philippine Duchesne as the patron saint of those embarking on second careers (as is the case for many catechetical leaders and catechists today). Perhaps even more important is her witness as a woman who prayed always.

Legend says that Native American children sneaked behind her as she knelt and sprinkled bits of paper on her habit; they came back hours later to find them undisturbed. Our learners will see our attentiveness when we pray with them, our participation when they see us at liturgy, and so on. Yet, how will they know we are people rooted in continual prayer? We are called not just to pray prayers (as important as that is) but to be prayerful people. A prayerful life spills into all we are and do. People (our learners) can spot the signs of prayerful people: gratitude, hope, patience, compassion and care, and a deep respect for each person.

Wonderings to Ponder and Live Today
- What atmosphere might be set if, at the beginning of each session, we and our learners prayed that the time together would be enveloped in prayer, feeling grateful to be gathered with and in God's love?
- At the conclusion of each session, pray in gratitude for all that happened, thanking God for the ways God worked compassionately through you.
- What types of prayer forms help you to live prayerfully all the time? What types of new prayer forms might you share with your learners?
- Let your learners (and their families) know that you are praying for them. Send them a note with your prayer for them.

Sr. Thea Bowman

The U.S. bishops endorsed the sainthood cause of Sr. Thea Bowman in 2018. During her short lifetime (52 years), she was eager to learn from other cultures and wanted to share the abundance of her African American culture and spirituality. Sr. Thea became an evangelizer, teacher, writer, and singer, sharing the gospel and her rich cultural heritage throughout the nation.

Born on December 29, 1937, in Yazoo City, Mississippi, Thea was raised Protestant until she asked her parents if she could become a Catholic when she was nine years old. She was attracted to the church because of how Catholics seemed to love and care for one another, especially the poor and needy.

At 15, she joined the Franciscan Sisters of Perpetual Adoration, leaving Mississippi to move to the unfamiliar town of LaCrosse, Wisconsin, where she was the only African American member of her religious community.

After 16 years of teaching at the elementary, secondary, and university level, she was invited by the bishop of Jackson, Mississippi, to become the consultant for intercultural awareness for the diocese. In this role, Sr. Thea gave presentations across the country, combining singing, gospel preaching, prayer, and storytelling. Her programs were designed to break down racial and cultural barriers.

Devastating challenges came in 1984: both her parents died, and Thea was diagnosed with breast cancer. She vowed to "live until I die," continuing her rigorous speaking schedule. From her wheelchair, she addressed the U.S. bishops at their June 1989 meeting. Sr. Thea spoke to them as a sister having a "heart-to-heart" conversation with her brothers. At the end, she invited the bishops to move together, cross arms, and sing with her "We Shall Overcome."

An Inspiring Mentor for Us Today

One of Sr. Thea's unique gifts to us is her appreciation of how God created: a world of diversity. In a 1984 National Catholic Educational Association essay about the richness of diversity, she wrote, "If I begin to believe that we are all alike, look at what I'm going to miss: the richness, beauty, wholeness, and harmony of what God has created."

As catechists today, we have the continual opportunity to teach about the power of diversity as well as being witnesses of respect for the uniqueness of everyone—the type of witness that attracted Thea Bowman to the church.

Wonderings to Ponder and Live Today

- Are we aware of which cultures our learners come from? Do we know what traditions, customs, and values are important to these cultures?
- Research shows that all of us absorb what we see around us. In your meeting space, do you have posters/religious art representing all cultures?
- Invite visitors/parishioners who reflect diverse backgrounds to join you (as storytellers, helpers, etc.).
- Use literature that introduces learners to various cultures (one resource is Teaching Tolerance: www.tolerance.org/magazine/archives).
- Be careful of language.
    » Never let anyone repeat jokes that target people or groups.
    » Be aware of words, images, and situations that stereotype people of certain ethnic backgrounds (for instance, referring to children from a particular culture as "well-dressed," suggesting that this is an exception).

Mentors from Our Recent Past

We have reflected on some (of the many) saints officially recognized by the church who inspire us to teach and live the Good News. We are blessed abundantly because we also stand on the shoulders of giants from recent years who have influenced, guided, and deepened the ministry of catechesis for today.

This litany names just a few of them. As you reflect on their lives and contributions, you may wish to pray after each one, "Guide us"; "Inspire us"; "Be with us"; or "Pray for us."

Sr. Maria de la Cruz Aymes

- who authored several religious education programs for children, beginning with the *On Our Way Series* (1957–62), and then worked to update it with the vision of Vatican II
- who, in her later years, worked for pluralism and enculturation in the church while a member of the National Advisory Committee on Adult Religious Education (NACARE)...

Dr. Christiane Brusselmans

- whose efforts for the restoration of the RCIA contributed to the establishment of the catechumenate in many parishes in the U.S. and in other countries
- whose vision, determination, and belief in the vocation of the laity and the importance of the family in the mission of the church still impact us today...

Sofia Cavalletti
- who developed the Catechesis of the Good Shepherd, an approach to religious education that aims to help children have "a living encounter with the living God"
- who, through her methods, emphasized reflection, contemplation, meditation, awe, wonder, and mystery for children's formation...

Joanne Chafe
- who, from an early age, worked for thirty-seven years in the National Office of Religious Education of the Canadian Conference of Catholic Bishops
- who was a leader in the development of adult faith formation as she served as president of the Religious Education Association of the United States and Canada and as president of the International Forum on Adult Religious Education...

Françoise Darcy-Bérubé
- who, named by some as "one of the great Mothers of Catholic catechetics," was the principal author of *Come to the Father*, the first elementary school religious curriculum for American Catholic children written in the spirit of the Second Vatican Council
- who believed that "an authentic Christian initiation of children is inseparable from the evangelization and spiritual care of the parents, whatever their lifestyle and according to their degree of readiness"...

Pierre Teilhard de Chardin, SJ
- who influenced catechetics and theology because of his work in bringing science, religion, and mysticism together
- who, through his writings, deepened our understandings of ecology, interfaith encounters, the unification of humanity, the place of love in creating greater unity, and the central importance of spirituality and mysticism in religious life...

James J. DiGiacomo
- who helped reshape Catholic religious education, especially the faith formation of adolescents, in the post-Vatican II era
- who made important contributions to the development of youth ministry and to adult religious education...

Sr. Catherine Dooley, OP
- who developed liturgical catechesis, which acknowledges the liturgy as a source for catechesis, leading communities and individuals to full, active, and conscious faith in the light of instruction and the experience of Christian living
- who advocated that the formation of catechists should have a catechetical style culminating not in theology or method but in a life of witness and mission...

Fr. Jim Dunning
- who, with indefatigable energy, fascinating creativity, and committed ministry, pioneered the implementation of the Rite of Christian Initiation of Adults (RCIA) and was founding director of the North American Forum on the Catechumenate
- who was named *Indabaye Nkosi*, "God's story," by the people of South Africa who learned God's story because of the stories that punctuated his homilies and teaching...

Sr. Mariella Fye and Msgr. Wilfrid Paradis
- who organized the largest consultation ever undertaken in U.S. Catholic religious education, seeking perspectives from scholars and constituencies across cultural, ethnic, racial, educational, and ecumenical boundaries
- who used this consultation to produce the first U.S. National Catechetical Directory, *Sharing the Light of Faith* (1979)...

Maria Harris
- who, as a prolific writer, speaker, and advocate of religious education, helped us to see the connections among religious education, justice, aesthetics, and spirituality
- who, in helping us understand "curriculum" as more than a set of printed materials, insisted that the church is itself a curriculum...

Sr. José Hobday
- a Seneca woman who, growing up on a reservation in Colorado and chosen by her tribe at the age of seven to be a storyteller, continued that storytelling in her catechesis around the world for her entire life
- who taught us that we have much to learn from Native American spirituality, including how to make prayer more creation-centered, how to have a greater appreciation of the connection between the living and the dead, how to love and respect silence and cherish solitude, and how to place a greater emphasis on celebration...

Fr. Johannes Hofinger

- who, at times called the father of modern catechetics, urged catechists to develop a passion for our faith tradition and helped us learn how to engage others with its riches
- who, as a theologian and international authority on multicultural catechesis, was one of the theologians who established the intellectual foundation for the Second Vatican Council, directly influencing three of its consequential documents...

Jane Wolford Hughes

- who, appointed by Cardinal John Dearden as the first executive director of adult education for the Archdiocese of Detroit during the 1960s, was one of the first women to hold a significant diocesan position
- who, in designing multitudinous archdiocesan adult programs and listening sessions, believed they must spring from the needs of the people and that the facilitators/teachers must be formed, prepared, and open to creative methods of making faith formation available to everyone...

Bishop Raymond Lucker

- who, as a pioneer in the national movement to reform Catholic education, believed strongly that catechesis is for conversion
- who advocated continually that the most important form of religious education is that which aims at strengthening the faith of adults...

Janaan Manternach and Carl J. Pfeiffer
- who, as assistant directors at the National Confraternity of Christian Doctrine Center (in the 1960s), an office of the United States Catholic Conference, were asked to write a children's catechetical series to replace the widely used Baltimore Catechism
- who, in their Life, Love, Joy series (and numerous other writings and workshops), invited children and families to reflect on their life experience in dialogue with the faith of the Catholic tradition...

Fr. Berard Marthaler, OFM, Conv.
- who, recognized by many as a mentor, astute critic, and sage, taught a generation of catechetical leaders at Catholic University of America and was the editor of the national catechetical quarterly *The Living Light* for more than thirty years
- who, with a reputation for always thinking ahead, missing nothing, and making connections among the disciplines, promoted critical thinking about the church's task of handing on the faith in the 21st century, especially convinced that "Catechesis Isn't Just for Children Anymore" (a chapter in a 1997 book)...

Jack McBride
- whose mission, passion, and work of his career was the evangelization and faith formation of adults
- whose creativity and insights contributed to a leader's discussion guide for the document *Adult Catechesis in the Christian Community* and a leader's guide to the U.S. bishops' pastoral letter on adult faith formation, *Our Hearts Were Burning within Us*...

Sister Anne Marie Mongoven, OP
- who made significant contributions to the field of catechesis as associate director of religious education in Madison, Wisconsin, and, while at Santa Clara University, created and taught in a holistically integrated catechetical program
- who co-authored a catechetical series for children, *Living Waters*, which started with human experience, deepening children's ability to connect their lives with the symbols of faith, bringing deeper meaning to their faith lives...

Dr. Gabriel Moran, AFSC
- who, as scholar, teacher, and author of over four hundred essays and thirty-one books, made significant contributions to the development of theology and religious education in the years following the Second Vatican Council
- who, with several others, published the *Alternative Religious Education* newsletter for forty-five years, inviting people to create new ways to meet today's needs...

Lee Nagel
- who served as diocesan director of Total Catholic Education (superintendent of schools and director of adult faith formation, youth ministry, and catechesis) for the diocese of Green Bay for more than fifteen years and as executive director of the National Conference of Catechetical Leaders
- who, as a catechist, retreat leader, and author, taught as Jesus did: through stories, weaving together the elements of people's lives in ways that made the message of Jesus and an all-loving, all-caring, all-forgiving God alive in the minds of those who heard him...

Mary Perkins Ryan

- who, as a laywoman and pioneer in liturgical and catechetical reform movements, was the founding executive editor of *The Living Light* and editor of *Professional Approaches for Christian Educators* (PACE), the first catechetical journal to address both the professional and practical aspects of religious education
- who, as a leading voice for professional standards in parish faith formation, insisted that educating in faith must be understood as educating to "a religious way of life" rather than merely "teaching about religion"...

Fr. Gerard S. Sloyan

- who, as an author, lecturer, professor, and scholar, was a leader in religious education, New Testament, liturgy, ecumenism, and interreligious dialogue and a mentor to many in the field of catechetics
- who, challenging the caliber and impact of religious instruction based exclusively on the question-and-answer method, argued that the task of catechesis was to respond to the important questions alive in the minds and hearts of the learners...

Inspiring Mentors for You

Each of us is unique: as God's creation and in the ways we live our ministry as catechists. In this way, we all are attracted to specific well-known mentors as well as having mentors from our lives—family, friends, parishioners, neighbors—all of whom guide us and inspire us. Take time periodically to use the following suggestions in your prayer time to reflect on those saints and mentors for you and your catechetical ministry.

Music: "Litany of the Saints": https://www.youtube.com/watch?v=kId0NBvNiCk

Scripture Reading: Hebrews 12:1–2

Reflection
- Which of the canonized saints of our church inspire me in my ministry as catechist?
- How might I live their commitment to spreading the Good News in my times today?

Scripture Reading: 1 Corinthians 12:27–28

Reflection
- Who are the people in my life (both living and deceased) who have shown me what it means to be a follower of Jesus?
- Who are the former catechists in my family, my parish, my (arch)diocese (both living and deceased)? With those who are still living, how often do I talk with them? Have I invited them to be guest catechists with my learners?

Scripture Reading: Isaiah 30:21

Reflection
- Who is mentoring and inspiring me right now? What am I learning from them?
- How often do I thank them?

Music: "You Raise Me Up": https://www.youtube.com/watch?v=TRcIEMgppK8

Another Suggestion for Prayer

Sr. José Hobday, OSF, an author and international speaker on prayer and spirituality, spoke of a prayer method she used while praying alone (yet also praying within the community of saints). José imagined herself as part of a large circle. Within the circle, she visualized many people: wisdom figures within the community (past and present), people who were important to her, people who had connections with her. She prayed in the presence of, and with the support of, all these people.

Reflection
- Especially as I reflect on my ministry as catechist, who is within my circle: my family and relatives; patron saints of catechists; the patron saints of my learners; the families, especially the ancestors, of my learners; all those who have mentored me?
- How might I invite my learners to pray within a circle of those who guide and inspire them?